THE WASHINGTON P
LITTLE BOOK O

Other "Little Book of Wisdom" Titles Available

THE WASHINGTON BASEBALL FAN'S LITTLE BOOK OF WISDOM

Frederic J. Frommer

TAYLOR TRADE PUBLISHING

Lanham • New York • Dallas • Boulder • Toronto • Oxford

THE WASHINGTON BASEBALL FAN'S LITTLE BOOK OF WISDOM
Copyright © 2005 by Frederic J. Frommer

This Taylor Trade Publishing paperback edition of *The Washington Baseball Fan's Little Book of Wisdom* is an original publication. It is published by arrangement with the author.

Published by Taylor Trade Publishing
An imprint of The Rowman & Littlefield Publishing Group, Inc.
4501 Forbes Boulevard, Suite 200, Lanham, Maryland 20706

Distributed by NATIONAL BOOK NETWORK

Library of Congress Cataloging-in-Publication Data

Frommer, Frederic J.
The Washington baseball fan's little book of wisdom / Frederic J. Frommer.
p. cm.
ISBN 1-58979-275-0 (pbk. : alk. paper)
1. Baseball—Washington (D.C.)—History. 2. Washington Senators (Baseball
team : 1886–1960) 3. Washington Senators (Baseball team : 1961–1971)
4. Washington Nationals (Baseball team: 2005–) I. Title.
GV863.W18F76 2005   796.357'64'09753—dc22   2005000809

Manufactured in the United States of America.

To my father, Harvey, who once dedicated a book to me
with the hope that I'd one day return the favor.
His inspiration and coaching has made that possible.

• Introduction •

When Washington, D.C., was finally awarded the Montreal Expos in 2004, the question of what to rename them became, of course, a political question. Some traditionalists wanted to name them for the original Washington Senators, but D.C. Mayor Anthony Williams didn't like the idea.

"We don't have senators here," he said, referring to the city's lack of voting representation in Congress. "Give us two senators, and I'll be happy to call them the Senators." The mayor liked the name Grays, in honor of the Negro League's Homestead Grays, who had split their time between Pittsburgh and D.C. in the late 1930s and 1940s. That would also have given Williams some credit with the city's black voters.

In the end, Major League Baseball, which still owned the team, settled on Nationals. This had actually been the official name of the original team all the way through the 1950s, but fans referred to them as the Senators. The team finally recognized this and changed the name to Senators in 1956.

Nationals makes more sense now that the team is in the National League, instead of the American League, where the old team played. Still, baseball should have selected a name more in keeping with the city's culture: the Lobbyists, the Bureaucrats, the Climbers, the Flaks. A friend even suggested the Deputy Assistant Undersecretaries. OK, maybe that's *too* inside-the-beltway.

But another description comes to mind when you mention Washington baseball: futility.

For generations of Washington Senators fans, their team was defined by losing. There was a Broadway show celebrating the team's haplessness (*Damn Yankees*) and a national slogan mocking them ("First in war, first in peace, and last in the American League").

The first version of the Washington Senators, which played from 1901 to 1960, won just one World Series title and three pennants. But perhaps worse, the team left town just before it got good.

After moving to Minnesota and becoming the Twins, the franchise, stocked with great players, quickly became competitive. Powered by former Senators

Harmon Killebrew and Bob Allison, the Twins won three division titles and an American League pennant in their first decade in the Twin Cities.

Sure, Washington got a replacement team, the Senators II, in 1961. But if anything, that team was even worse than the old Senators. It finished in last place four times and second-to-last three times, with just one lonely winning season in its 11 years before shuttling off to Texas in 1972. At least the Texas Rangers had the decency to finish dead last in their first two seasons, before bolting to a second-place finish under manager Billy Martin in 1974.

Futility continued for Washington after losing its second team. Several times, Washington was close to landing an expansion team or luring a team from another city, but each time it came up empty. When Major League Baseball targeted two teams for extinction after the 2001 season, one was a former Washington team (the Minnesota Twins) while the other was a future Washington team (the Montreal Expos).

Washingtonians couldn't help but ask: Can't we just have the Twins back? The Twins went on to win three straight division titles after baseball's ill-fated contraction plan. Returning them to Washington just as they were getting good would have repaid a city that lost an up-and-coming team to Minnesota 40 years earlier.

Alas, Washington was forced to settle for the Expos. A scrappy bunch, no doubt, but one that had been recently stripped of talented players such as Orlando Cabrera, Vladimir Guerrero, Javier Vazquez, Bartolo Colon, and Carl Pavano. The 2004 Expos finished in last place, familiar ground for a Washington team.

But the Washington Senators were not some long, national nightmare. There were a few great seasons through the years, and many great players. Topping the list was Walter Johnson, who held the all-time strikeout record until Nolan Ryan broke it decades later. Johnson's model behavior would be welcome in today's steroid-polluted era. He didn't smoke or drink, and his strongest expression was "Goodness gracious sakes alive."

Other Washington Hall-of-Famers include outfielders Harmon Killebrew, Sam Rice, Goose Goslin, Heinie Manush; infielder Joe Cronin; catcher Rick Ferrell; and pitcher Early Wynn.

Clark Griffith helped turn around the moribund Senators team after taking over as manager in 1912. The team had been in the American League for 11 seasons and had yet to play over .500. Griffith led the team to four straight winning seasons, then bought controlling interest of the team in 1920. Griffith hired 27-year-old Bucky Harris as manager in 1924, and "The Boy Wonder" led the team to its only World Series title that season, and another pennant the next year.

A decade later, Griffith installed 26-year-old shortstop Joe Cronin as manager and was rewarded with yet another pennant in 1933. After a seventh-place finish the next year, however, Griffith sold Cronin—who was his son-in-law— to the Boston Red Sox for $250,000 and brought back Harris as manager.

And that was about it for the glory years. Washington managed a couple of second-place finishes during World War II, coming within 1½ games of winning the pennant in 1945, but after that, they would never finish higher than fourth place.

That lack of competitive teams doomed Washington attendance for years, ultimately costing the city two teams. The original Senators would never draw more than one million fans after 1946 and finished dead-last in American League attendance their last six seasons before moving to Minnesota. It was more of the same with the second Senators team, which finished in the bottom third of the league in attendance every year except for 1969.

The low attendance history also hurt the city's efforts to regain a team, but much has changed in Washington in the past three decades. The D.C. region, including its suburbs, has become one of the most affluent in the nation. The team picked up 10,000 season ticket deposits even before Major League Baseball officially approved the relocation of the Expos. A baseball-starved city, having lost two teams already, will surely hold on to this one.

Come Up with a Better Slogan

Washington finished in the American League cellar 13 times,
leading to the famous expression "First in war, first in peace,
and last in the American League."

Believe in Reincarnation

In 1961, the Senators moved to Minnesota where they became
the Minnesota Twins. But the American League immediately
awarded one of two expansion franchises to the nation's capital,
which became the second incarnation of the Washington Senators.

Last One Out, Take Home Plate

The Washington Senators were forced to forfeit their last game ever, played on September 30, 1971. Fans rushed out onto the field of RFK Stadium with two outs in the top of the 9th inning and the Senators leading the New York Yankees, 7-5. New York was awarded the game by the traditional forfeit score of 9-0.

Stand Up for Your Rights . . .

Soon after announcing the Montreal Expos would be moving to
Washington, Major League Baseball decided to name the team the
Nationals, the original name of the American League team that
played in Washington before changing its name to the Senators in
the mid-1950s. Mayor Anthony Williams, who helped bring baseball
back to Washington, objected to naming the team the Senators
because the city has no representation in Congress.

. . . but Be Willing to Compromise

"The Mayor was on Grays. Bud [Selig] was on Senators.
I think you see a compromise candidate. But I don't want
to sell it as that. I think it's a great name."
—Expos, er, Nationals President Tony Tavares

Keep Your Uniform—
It Might Be Worth Something

Montreal Expos first baseman Brad Wilkerson toured with a team
of U.S. All-Stars in November 2004, after the Expos were awarded
to Washington. Wilkerson wore his Montreal Expos uniform on
the tour, making him the last Expos player. His agent, Scott Boras,
said Wilkerson was like a "cult figure."

Put Your Money Down Early

Even before Major League Baseball officially approved the move
of the Montreal Expos to Washington, the team picked up over
10,000 deposits for season tickets for the 2005 season at RFK Stadium.
That translated to 812,000 game-day tickets, more than the Expos
drew the entire 2004 season in Montreal and San Juan.

Put Your Soul into Baseball

So awful were the Washington Senators that they even inspired
a novel about a fan who agrees to sell his soul to the Devil in exchange
for the chance to lead his beloved Senators to a pennant over the
New York Yankees. The book was adapted into the
1950s Broadway play *Damn Yankees*.

Give Me the Short Version

A Hall of Fame manager started his playing career as a catcher
for a short-lived National League Washington team in the late 1880s.
His full name was Cornelius McGillicuddy, but sportswriters
shortened his name to Connie Mack.

You Can Only Teach So Much

Ted Williams, perhaps the best hitter in baseball history,
took over as manager of the Senators in 1969. He got off to a great start,
leading a team that had finished in last place the year before to an
86-76 record, but the team had losing seasons under Williams in
1970 and 1971, the franchise's last two years in Washington.

Life Isn't Fair

In the team's last season in Washington, 1960, the Senators finished
in seventh place out of eight teams. But they soon turned things around
in Minnesota as the renamed Twins, zooming to a second-place finish
in 1962 and an American League pennant in 1965.

Not Everyone's a Baseball Fan

At the official unveiling of the team's new name and logo in 2004, following its move to Washington, a protester jumped on the stage and yelled, "This is a bad deal, people!" Several people wrestled him off the stage, including Charlie Brotman, a longtime public address announcer for the Washington Senators.

Don't Waste Any Time

Just two weeks into his job as general manager of the Washington
baseball team (it didn't yet have a new name), Jim Bowden made
a series of moves to make the former Expos more competitive.
He signed free agents shortstop Cristian Guzman and third baseman
Vinny Castilla, and traded for Angels outfielder Jose Guillen.

Let the Fans Decide

Washington was one of the original eight teams when the American
League started play in 1901. The team called itself the Nationals,
partly to avoid confusion with the defunct Washington Senators National
League team that folded after the 1899 season. But fans continued
to call the new team the Senators, and the franchise finally
acknowledged the popular sentiment by officially changing
the name of the team to Senators in 1956.

You Gotta Have a lot of Little Boy to Manage This Game . . .

Washington player–manager Bucky Harris, a second baseman, led the team to its only World Series championship in 1924. Harris, 27 at the time, was known as "The Boy Wonder." He managed the team for three periods: 1924–28, 1935–42, and 1950–55.

. . . and Youth Can Be a Winning Formula

All three Senators pennants came when the team's manager was under 30. Harris led the team to back-to-back pennants in 1924 and 1925, and in 1933, Washington won its final pennant with 26-year-old player–manager Joe Cronin, a shortstop.

Don't Quit Your Night Job

Washington was home to a baseball-playing spy in the 1930s.
Moe Berg, the team's third-string catcher, traveled to Japan to play
on an all-star team, but his real mission was to take espionage photos.
Berg was a brilliant mathematician and linguist but just a
.243 lifetime hitter, prompting this line: "He can speak
12 languages but can't hit in any of them."

Value Diversity . . .

Until 1947, major league baseball was off limits to black players,
but Washington did not miss out on great black baseball talent.
From the late 1930s to the 1940s, the Homestead Grays of the Negro
National League split their time between Pittsburgh and Washington.
Featuring stars such as Josh Gibson and Buck Leonard, the Grays
were clearly Washington's superior team, winning nine
league championships from 1938 to 1948.

. . . and Fight Prejudice

In 1941, Senators owner Clark Griffith secretly met with Gibson
and Leonard to discuss signing the stars to major league contracts.
But baseball officials found out about the meeting and
ordered Griffith to break off negotiations.

What Goes Around Comes Around

Some joke that Washington got President George W. Bush
as compensation for losing its baseball team. The Senators left
to become the Texas Rangers after the 1971 season, and Bush became
the team's managing general partner in 1989. He became
president in 2001, bringing a baseball perspective—
although not a team—to the nation's capital.

Learn to Overcome Adversity

In the late 1880s, a deaf-mute rookie burst onto the scene
for the Washington Senators. William E. Hoy, also known as
"Dummy Hoy," led the National League with 82 stolen bases in his
first season and finished his career with 597 steals. Legend has it
that umpires first started using hand signals because he could
not hear the calls. Hoy was 5'4" and weighed just 148 pounds.

Watch That Pitch, Mr. President

Throwing out the first ball at Washington's home opener was a long tradition among presidents, starting with William Howard Taft in 1910. President Franklin D. Roosevelt threw out eight season-openers, once missing his target so badly—or did he?—that he nailed a photographer.

The Comet Launches
One into Orbit

On April 17, 1953, Yankee slugger Mickey Mantle crushed a ball
565 feet, over the bleachers at Griffith Stadium. The shot came off
Washington pitcher Chuck Stobbs, pacing a 7-3 New York victory.

Don't Rush to Print

Just three years after the expansion Senators moved to Texas,
Washington almost got another team to replace them in the
National League. A supermarket owner made a deal to buy the
San Diego Padres and move them to D.C. for the 1974 season,
and Topps even printed baseball cards of Padres players with
"Washington" written on them. But the deal fell through, and
McDonald's founder Ray A. Kroc bought the team
and kept it in San Diego.

Two Are Better Than One

On May 26, 1930, Senators Goose Goslin and Joe Judge hit back-to-back home runs twice in the same game, the first time that feat had been accomplished in the twentieth century. The four homers helped Washington beat the Yankees, 10-7.

Don't Sit on a Lead . . .

In 1928, Washington Senators outfielder Goose Goslin held
a one-point lead in the race for the American League batting title
with just one at-bat left in the final game of the season. Goslin was
set to skip the at-bat to preserve his lead, but his teammates shamed
him into staying in the game. After an unsuccessful attempt to get
thrown out of the game by arguing with the umpire, Goslin got an
infield hit and finished the season with a .379 average, one point
ahead of Heinie Manush of the St. Louis Browns.

. . . because No Job Is Safe

Two years later, Goslin was traded to the Browns for Manush,
who helped lead the Senators to an American League pennant in 1933,
the last in franchise history. Manush led the league in hits and triples,
and finished second in batting (again) with a .336 average.

Be Ready to Wait for a Winner

After joining the American League in 1901, the Senators
went on to have losing records in their first 11 seasons, including
four last-place finishes and five second-to-last finishes.

Swing for the White House

Government clerks started up a baseball club, the Potomacs,
in Washington in 1859. A second team, the Nationals, was formed
later that year. In 1860, the Potomacs beat the Nationals in a spot that is
now a popular Washington place for recreational softball—the Ellipse,
located behind the White House.

Walk, Don't Run

On September 11, 1949, Senators pitchers walked
11 Yankees batters in one inning, a major league record.
Overall, Washington walked 17 men, and lost 20-5 at Yankee Stadium.

31

"I told him that I wanted to be a real major league baseball player, a genuine professional like Honus Wagner. My friend said that he'd like to be President of the United States."

—President Dwight David Eisenhower, recalling a childhood conversation growing up in Kansas

"By bringing the baseball pennant to Washington you have made the National Capital more truly the center of worthy and honorable national aspirations."

—President Calvin Coolidge, at a parade welcoming the Washington Senators after they clinched the 1924 pennant

Don't Try This Yourself

In 1908, Washington Senators catcher Charles "Gabby" Street caught a ball tossed from the top of the Washington Monument in full catcher's gear. The ball was sold at a World War I bonds auction for $40,000.

It's a Team Game

In 1909, Walter Johnson posted a 2.22 ERA, but still
wound up losing nearly twice as many games as he won.
Johnson finished with a 13-25 won-lost record.

Good Deeds Are
Not Always Reciprocated

In 1953, the Senators agreed to allow an American League
team into its region, paving the way for the St. Louis Browns
to become the Baltimore Orioles the following season. But a
half-century later, Orioles owner Peter Angelos did everything
he could to block a team from returning to Washington.

Keep Your Fans Entertained

Decades before baseball mascots like the San Diego Chicken
and the Phillie Phanatic, Washington offered its fans the comedy
duo of Al Schacht and Nick Altrock, two coaches who teamed
up to entertain fans before games. Schacht would be
known as "The Clown Prince of Baseball."

Treasure Every Base Runner

On June 23, 1917, Washington's Ray Morgan led off the game
with a walk against Boston pitcher Babe Ruth, who was promptly
ejected for arguing with the umpire. Morgan was thrown out
trying to steal off reliever Ernie Shore, who went on to retire
the next 26 batters in Boston's 4-0 win.

Families Should Stay Together . . .

In 1937 and 1938, the Ferrell brothers
teamed up as battery-mates in Washington after doing
the same for the Boston Red Sox the previous three seasons.
Rick, a Hall of Fame catcher, called signals for his younger brother, Wes.

. . . but Sometimes, Business Is Business

Washington owner Calvin Griffith sold his own son-in-law, player–manager Joe Cronin, to the Boston Red Sox for $250,000.

Quit While You're Behind

Once, Washington's Walter Johnson got two quick strikes
on Cleveland's Ray Chapman. The Indians batter chucked his bat
and headed back to the dugout. When the umpire told him he
had only two strikes, Chapman quipped, "I know, and you
can have the next one. It won't do me any good."

Know When to Quit

Major League Baseball made the move of the Montreal Expos official
with a vote on December 3, 2004. The tally was 29-1, with the only
dissenting vote coming from Baltimore Orioles owner Peter Angelos,
who argued a Washington team would cost him fans.

You're Only As Good As Your Word . . .

After Senators owner Clark Griffith died in 1955,
Griffith's nephew and adopted son, Calvin Griffith, took over
the team. In 1958, Calvin Griffith told Senators stockholders:
"The team will not be shifted out of this city in my lifetime."
He moved the team to Minneapolis in 1961.

. . . and Sometimes, It's Better to Say Nothing

In 1978, Calvin Griffith angered many when he said of the move to Minneapolis: "Black people don't go to ballgames, but they'll fill up a rassling ring and put up such a chant they'll scare you to death. We came here because you've got good, hardworking white people here." The *Minneapolis Star* ran a front-page editorial calling on him to sell the team.

Better Late Than Never

Montreal Expos manager Frank Robinson came with the team
when it relocated to Washington, fulfilling a long-delayed stint
in the nation's capital. He had been the choice to manage a
Washington franchise in 1974, before a deal to move the
San Diego Padres to the nation's capital fell through.

Prepare for Life after Baseball

Washington's catcher in the 1920s, Muddy Ruel, went on to become
a lawyer after his playing career. He's the only major league baseball
player admitted to practice law before the U.S. Supreme Court.

Be Ready to Pitch . . .

Washington Hall of Fame outfielder Sam Rice actually made his debut
as relief pitcher for the Senators in a game against the Chicago White Sox
in 1915. Rice finished his career with a .322 batting average and
holds the team record for hits, runs, doubles, and triples.

. . . and to Field

In the same game, pitcher Walter Johnson started
in right field for injured regular Danny Moeller.
Johnson could handle the bat pretty well. He finished
with a lifetime batting average of .235 with 24 home runs.

Know Your Strengths

Washington infielder Eddie Foster, just 5'6" and 145 pounds,
played nearly 1,500 games and hit only a half-dozen homers.
But he was a prized contact hitter and was considered
a master of the hit-and-run play.

Know Your Limits

Hall-of-Famer Ed Delahanty was killed in his second season
with the Senators. The team suspended Delahanty, a heavy drinker,
for missing a game in 1903. A few days later, he was kicked
off a train near Niagara Falls after threatening riders.
His body was found in the Niagara River a week later.

Seek Perfection

Walter Johnson once shut out the New York Yankees three
times in four days. He would have probably pitched a fourth shutout,
but for the fact that there was no baseball played on Sundays back then.

Nothing Beats Being There

In Washington's only World Series championship, fans who couldn't make it to the ballpark got to watch the action, sort of, at the *Washington Post* building downtown. The paper erected a magnetic board with a baseball diamond that simulated the action.

Keep the Faith

In the 1990s, Washington came close to getting
a baseball team several times. It was a candidate for an
expansion team and, in 1996, the Houston Astros considered
moving to a Washington suburb in Northern Virginia.

Don't Let 'Em See You Cry

Just 4,768 fans came out to see the final game of the original
Washington Senators, a 2-1 loss to the Baltimore Orioles at
Griffith Stadium in 1960, before the team moved to Minneapolis.

Learn from Your Opponents

After a Cuban pitcher shut out the Senators in relief in the final game of the 1933 World Series, Washington owner Clark Griffith sent scout "Papa" Joe Cambria to look for baseball talent on the Caribbean island. Cambria helped develop a pipeline of Cuban players for the Senators.

Anything's Possible

In 1923, the Senators finished with a .490 winning percentage,
in fourth place, 23½ games behind the first-place New York Yankees.
But they won an improbable pennant the following season,
finishing with a .597 percentage, two games ahead of the Yankees.

You Don't Have to Hit Home Runs . . .

The Senators hit just 22 home runs in 1924, dead last in the
American League, even as they won their first pennant.
The home run total was less than half of Babe Ruth's 46.

. . . if You Have Good Pitching

That same year, Washington paced the American League
with a 3.35 ERA. Ace Walter Johnson led the league
in wins (23), ERA (2.72), and strikeouts (158).

Please, Hold the Mayo

Washington infielder Gil Torres hit into triple plays in
consecutive seasons—and both were started by Detroit
second baseman Eddie Mayo. On July 20, 1945, Torres hit a
line drive at Mayo, who turned the putout into a triple-killing.
On May 8, 1946, Mayo caught a deflected Torres line drive off
pitcher Hal Newhouser to start another triple play.

It's Good to Have Supporters

"I had cheerleaders there at Griffith Stadium. I didn't have to worry about name-calling. You got cheers from those people when you walked out onto the field. They'd let you know they appreciated you were there."
—Cleveland Indians outfielder Larry Doby, the first black player in the American League, on playing in Washington
(1997 *Washington Post* interview)

You've Got to Support the Home Team

Washington drew its smallest crowd at Griffith Stadium
on September 7, 1954, when just 460 fans came to watch
the home team beat the Philadelphia Athletics, 5-4.

Everyone Can Use a Fresh Start

The expansion Senators drew a Washington record 42,143 fans
at the new District of Columbia Stadium (later renamed RFK Stadium)
on April 9, 1962. Bernie Daniels, the winning pitcher, had lost the
last game ever played at old Griffith Stadium the year before.

Know Your Value . . .

Babe Ruth's 1931 salary was $80,000, topping President
Herbert Hoover's $75,000. When asked about making more than
the president, Ruth said, "Why not? I had a better year than he did."

. . . and Save Your Collectibles

A baseball autographed by President Franklin Roosevelt that he threw
as the ceremonial first pitch at Griffith Stadium in 1941 sold for $17,255
at a 1998 auction. At the same auction, Babe Ruth's first home
run ball at Yankee Stadium, signed by the Babe, fetched $126,500.

Keep It in the Family

Senators pitchers surrendered home runs to Red Sox
brothers Billy and Tony Conigliaro at a game at Fenway Park
in 1970. Billy tagged Jim Hannan in the fourth,
and Tony took Joe Grzenda deep in the seventh.

65

Put Congress to Work

Hall-of-Famer Harmon Killebrew was scouted by a U.S. senator
from Idaho, Herman Welker, who urged Senators owner Clark Griffith
to take a look at the 17-year-old player. Killebrew was a wise investment:
he'd go on to hit 573 home runs for the Senators, Twins, and Royals.

Don't Be Afraid to Stretch Yourself

Some say the seventh-inning stretch was invented
in 1910 when President William Howard Taft stood
up in the seventh inning of a game in Washington.
Fans stood up with the 300-pound president out of respect.

"You can't make chicken salad out of chicken feathers."

—Quote attributed to Washington Senators manager Joe Kuhel after his team finished last in 1949. Turns out he probably used a more colorful word than "feathers."

Look for the Best

Senators owner Clark Griffith once tried to buy
Ty Cobb from the Detroit Tigers for $100,000.

Seek Divine Intervention

The Senators won their only World Series when a ground ball by
Washington's Earl McNeely hit a pebble and bounced over the head of
New York Giants third baseman Fred Lindstrom in the 12th inning
of Game 7. Muddy Ruel scored the winning run on the play.

It's Important to Be Well Rounded

Walter Johnson, one of the greatest pitchers of all time,
also holds the record for highest single-season batting average
for a pitcher. He hit a whopping .433 in 1925, with 20 RBIs.

Find Talent Where You Can

In 1944, Senators owner Clark Griffith plucked outfielder
Ed Boland from the New York Sanitation Department team.

Be in a Hurry . . .

Washington's Heinie Manush holds the record for the quickest 100 hits
in a season, hitting the mark in the 60th game of the 1934 season.
He would finish the year with 194 hits and a .349 batting average.

. . . but Don't Work Too Hard

Washington pitcher Dean Stone won the 1954 All-Star Game
without breaking a sweat. He came into the game in the eighth inning
with two outs, but didn't have to retire a batter as the National League's
Red Schoendienst was caught trying to steal home.

Sometimes, Nice Guys Finish First . . .

Hall of Fame pitcher Walter Johnson, a humble and gentle man,
had to wait until his 18th season before winning his only pennant,
in 1924. That season, at the age of 36, he went 23-7
and won the league's Most Valuable Player award.

. . . and Will Win Over the Fans

Johnson received an $8,000, seven-passenger Lincoln paid for by fans
at a ceremony at Griffith Stadium prior to the World Series opener.
"There is more genuine interest in him than there is in a presidential
election," Will Rogers wrote of Johnson in a column late that season.

Some People Are Just Talented

After retiring in 1927, Walter Johnson came back to manage
the team from 1929 to 1932. After an initial losing season,
Johnson guided the team to winning percentages of .610, .597,
and .604, although Washington failed to win a pennant.

Prejudice Never Pays

The Senators were one of the last teams to integrate. Their first black player, Cuban outfielder Carlos Paula, made his debut on September 6, 1954, more than seven years after Jackie Robinson broke baseball's color barrier in 1947. The Senators finished in the bottom half of the league each of those seasons.

Baseball Belongs in Washington . . .

When he wasn't saving the union, President Abraham Lincoln
liked to play baseball. An 1860 political cartoon shows
him vanquishing three opponents on a baseball field.

. . . but Political Support Is Necessary

Lincoln's successor, Andrew Johnson, gave the White House staff time off from work to attend a tournament featuring teams from Washington, Philadelphia, and Brooklyn.

Get It Right the First Time

The Senators won the longest opening-day game in
major league history when they beat the Philadelphia Athletics, 1-0,
in 15 innings on April 13, 1926. Walter Johnson, 38 years old,
went the distance, striking out 12 batters.

Sometimes a Team Needs New Blood

After starting out with 11 straight losing seasons
from 1901 to 1911, the Senators had four straight winning years
under new manager Clark Griffith. Known as the "Old Fox,"
Griffith would play an even more important role as owner,
putting together competitive teams with limited resources.

It's Good to Have Connections

In 1959, President Dwight Eisenhower attended a Senators game and called over Washington slugger Harmon Killebrew to sign a ball for his grandson, David. Killebrew asked for an autographed ball in return.

Go with a Hot Hand

In 1968, Washington slugger Frank Howard hit 10 home runs in a six-game period. He finished the year with 48 home runs in a season that was dominated by pitchers.

Be a Part of History

Babe Ruth finished his career with the New York Yankees in a series
at Washington. On September 29, 1934, he hit his last homer
as a Yankee; the next day, his last game in the American League,
he went hitless. Ruth went on to play briefly for the National League's
Boston Braves the next year before retiring two months into the season.

Take Chances

Senators pitcher George Mogridge stole home in the
12th inning of a game against the Chicago White Sox,
helping Washington to a 5-1 victory.

Hard Work Pays Off

Washington pitcher Tom Cheney set the major league record
for most strikeouts in a game, fanning 21 Orioles in a marathon
16-inning performance in 1962. The Senators won the game, 2-1.

"I did something wrong and it turned out to make me famous."

—Former Washington pitcher Paul Hopkins,
at his 99th birthday celebration in 2003, commenting on giving
up Babe Ruth's record-tying 59th home run in 1927 in his
major league debut. Hopkins was the oldest living major league
player before dying 10 months shy of his 100th birthday.

Aim High

Former Washington player–manager Joe Cronin went on to
become American League president in 1959. Two years later,
he oversaw a league expansion that added a team in Washington
to replace the original Senators, who had moved to Minneapolis.

Use What You've Got

Pitcher Stan Coveleski practiced pitching as a kid in rural
Pennsylvania in the late 1800s by throwing rocks at tin cans that hung
from trees. The Senators traded for him before the 1925 season, when
Coveleski was already 35, but it proved a wise pickup. The future
Hall-of-Famer went 20-5 and led the league with a 2.84 ERA.

Winning Isn't Everything . . .

Senators pitcher Pedro Ramos led the American League
in losses four straight years, from 1958 to 1961, covering the
team's last three seasons in Washington and first one in Minnesota.
He lost 18 games twice, 19 games once, and was a 20-game loser
for the Twins. Ramos actually didn't pitch that badly—his ERA
in that span ranged from a low of 3.45 to a high of 4.23.

. . . but It Sure Beats Losing

Ramos found success in New York, after the Yankees
picked him up in September 1964. He saved eight games with a
1.25 ERA during the stretch drive, helping the team win the pennant.
Ramos returned to Washington for his final big league
season to play for the expansion Senators in 1970.

Never Give Up

On May 14, 1914, the Senators were no-hit for nine innings
by White Sox pitcher Jim Scott, but won the game in the
10th inning on singles by Chick Gandil and Howard Shanks.

A Walk's As Good As a Hit

Washington third baseman Eddie Yost was known as the
"Walking Man." He led the American League in walks
six times and finished with 1,614 career walks.

Keep Coming Back for More

Pitcher Bobo Newsom had five tours of duty with the Washington
Senators over a 20-year career that began in 1929. He also pitched
for the Dodgers, Cubs, Browns, Red Sox, Tigers, Yankees, and Giants.

"This is the toughest clean-up hitting I've ever done."

—Former Washington great Harmon Killebrew at his 1984
Hall of Fame induction ceremony, commenting on following
Luis Aparicio, Pee Wee Reese, Don Drysdale, and fellow
Senators alum Rick Ferrell on the podium that day

Move in the Fences!

In 1945, the Senators' only home run at their home field,
Griffith Stadium, came on an inside-the-parker by Joe Kuhel. Despite
their lack of pop, the Senators were a pretty good team that year—
they finished in second place, just 1½ games behind the Detroit Tigers.

It's Good to Have Fans in High Places

After Washington's Mickey Vernon hit a 10th-inning home run
to win the opening-day game against the Yankees in 1954,
President Dwight Eisenhower was so excited that he started to make
his way to the field to congratulate him. Secret Service agents
intercepted the president and, instead, brought Vernon to Eisenhower's
box next to the Senators dugout. Vernon would go on to become the
first manager of the expansion Washington Senators team in 1961.

War Can Be Hell
on a Baseball Career

Washington shortstop Cecil Travis was one of the best hitting
shortstops of all time, batting .314 over 12 seasons with the Senators.
But he contracted frostbite on his feet while serving in the Army in
World War II, and when he returned to the team in 1945, he was never
the same player. Travis retired after the 1947 season at the age of 34.

Don't Be Afraid to Correct Your Mistakes

Washington traded shortstop Buddy Myer to the Boston Red Sox
for shortstop Topper Rigney in 1927. Rigney would be out of baseball
by the following season, while Myer would hit .313 with 30 stolen bases.
Washington traded back for him after the 1928 season. Myer,
who played mostly second base in his second stint, would hit at
least .300 seven more times, including a batting crown in 1935.

Everyone Needs a Good Nickname

Alvin "General" Crowder got his nickname from his namesake,
U.S. Army General Enoch Crowder. Crowder pitched with the
Senators from 1926 to 1927 and again from 1930 to 1934,
winning 24 games in 1933 to help the team win its third pennant.

• About the Author •

Frederic J. Frommer, 34, is a reporter with the Associated Press in Washington, D.C. Growing up in Queens, N.Y., his favorite sports were half-field baseball and street stickball. He graduated with a political science degree from Washington University in St. Louis in 1989 and got his master's degree in journalism from Columbia University in 1990. Frommer worked for six years at the (New Hampshire) *Valley News* before moving to Washington, D.C., in 1998. He has freelanced for, among others, the *Washington Post*, CNN, Knight Ridder, and washingtonpost.com.